AF438901

Introduction

There are a lot of methods where one can spend their money on the planet today, as everyone is seeking some return that will increase funds. Investors pick a financial investment which will bring a lot of advantages to them without costing them a lot money in the end. Investing in supplies is among the typical methods through which individuals are making some money out of their financial investments. There are various type of supplies to purchase as well as the usual ones are those that will certainly gain you a returns by the end of every year.

Rewards are a form of payment that are distributed to various capitalists from the business's earnings. This is typically done after the board of supervisors of that company determines as well as the reward is distributed according to the variety of shares a financier has in that company as well as the amount of profit the business has actually made. If you truly want to purchase dividend paying supplies, you need to recognize that not all business pay rewards to their financiers. Those that release out returns are the ones you ought to be purchasing.

There are several reasons why one would certainly purchase dividend paying supplies and a few of the most crucial ones are:

Stable repayments that the financier receives from the company

The possibility to reinvest back the dividend in order to boost their number of shares. This comes with numerous advantages in the long run

If this is your major interest in investing, this eBook must assist you on exactly how to delight in easy income from dividend financial investment returns.

Chapter 1: Dividend Stocks Basics

Earn money while you rest. This might seem like an impossibility, however it is precisely what you can expect when you buy reward supplies. This is since you make limited effort following your investment, and for the most part, you play a waiting video game to obtain returns. This revenue is separate from what you would certainly make in your income, which is why it is known as passive income. Returns supplies have actually been claimed to be one of one of the most powerful tools investors can make use of in order to build long term wide range. Below is an illustration of just how supply returns work:

If a firm you have purchased makes $2 billion in take-home pay annually, as well as it has about 100 million shares, then the profits per share will certainly be $20. If the business decides to pay only $10 per share as stock reward, and also keeps the other $10 for various other purposes, after that the firm will be stated to have a payment ratio of 50. The shareholders will certainly now appreciate both income as well as growth because business. Better yet, capitalists can reinvest their rewards back into the firm in order to expand their wide range quicker for much better returns in the future.

That buy stocks that pay dividends?

Dividends are basically one way that you can gain earnings, consequently individuals who have an interest in purchasing stocks that would certainly gain them some reward are these that are searching for a normal income. Consider the situation of individuals that have reached their retirement age. This group of individuals no more obtain an annual earnings as they utilized to when they were under employment, as a result they will certainly need some cash on a regular basis to be able to cover their personal expenditures as well as to pay some of their costs while at the same time having the ability to maintain their original investments in stock.

Other than senior citizens, young investors are additionally a group of people that are best fit for this kind of financial investment. What the young person will certainly do is not to pocket the dividend check for individual usage however to reinvest back the returns in order to expand their financial investment with time. This is what will allow them a chance to appreciate better reward returns in the future in life, when they will certainly want a constant income.

Selecting stocks that will pay rewards

There are a wide variety of alternatives that one can select from, for those investors that only intend to buy supplies that will certainly make them dividends. A good percent of firms in the country today and additionally on the planet pay returns to their investors, as a result you will certainly have an excellent listing of alternatives to choose from. The problem currently depends on exactly how one can set about making the ideal option. Like in anything else that you need to select, making the appropriate decision on the supplies to purchase is extremely essential. There are those stocks that are taken into consideration as excellent to invest in as well as there are those that may not offer you a good anticipated return.

Numerous financiers will definitely go with companies that pay a high reward to their shareholders, which is not a bad consideration in any way just that you need to go for a much more secure technique in your decision making. Consider business that have paid dividends regularly for a particular amount of time as an example, due to the fact that the opportunities that this fad will change are on the minimum. Since several financiers getting reward stocks are spending for the long-term, you have to ensure that at the very least every supply in your portfolio is providing something efficient completion of every quarter. It is always better to get something little but steady than obtaining a good reward this year but absolutely nothing in the coming years.

Bear in mind of the Dividend Aristocrat checklist. This is a very vital checklist as it includes firms that have paid rewards annually at the very least for the previous 25 years as well as which have actually raised dividends in at least one year in the 25 years.

The advantage regarding this list is that it is quickly accessible online and it is constantly upgraded each year. If you look for it today and the details it has will certainly help you make the finest selection of where to invest your cash, you are likely to obtain the right info.

You can likewise find a list of reward up-and-comers online or in the economic records. These are the companies that have a background of raising their dividends over time. Financial internet sites will certainly be the most effective areas to keep an eye out for an exact listing for much better choice production. If you select to spend in returns up-and-comers, you will certainly never go incorrect.

Points Worth Noting

Selecting a supply financial investment is a highly dangerous affair and also this likewise applies to buying supplies that will pay rewards. There is no guaranty that the firm whose stocks you have actually invested in will certainly pay you returns constantly, or after a few years. There is additionally no guarantee that the share price will rise. You just have to try your luck and hope that the selection that you have actually made will certainly work as per your strategies over time.

There are opportunities to minimize your danger that you can go with, as an example investing in extra traditional stocks. This can benefit you yet you will certainly have to manage decreased returns as well.

There are terms that you require to know as well, if you have actually currently chosen to begin buying reward stocks. Some of these are:

1. The Declaration Date: The day when a firm will certainly make a news about when a reward is to be paid.

2. Returns per Share: This is the dollar amount each share of stock obtains.

3.Ex-Dividend Date: This is the date prior to the investor should won their supply so regarding be able to take advantage of a reward.

4. The Dividend Yield: This is the dividend amount stated as a percentage of the marketplace rate of a share of the stock.

5. Dividend Reinvestment Plan: The firm makes a DRIP readily available so that investors are able to reinvest their returns instantly. This should enable them to purchase additional shares. It is very important for those financiers that wants to grow their investments.

Chapter 2: Investing in Dividend Stocks

With a long-term investment plan, perhaps for ten years or even more, your ideal type of investment ought to be reward stocks. What you need to do is to search for a range of costs supplies that pay rewards to buy. If you want to start developing your portfolio today, right here is an overview that will certainly take you through this to make sure that your returns over the long term are accomplished as well as to make sure that you are obtaining a returns earnings that you can rely on every year or every quarter.

Understand Yields from Dividend Stocks
Once you buy a supply, you anticipate development in the share price and also a reward return. This is what investors capitalize in so as to ensure that they are getting something terrific out of their financial investments. If as an example you invest in an organization with a returns return of 5% every year as well as its share rate rises by the same percentage, the overall annual return for you as an investor will certainly be 10%.
Constantly keep an eye out for reliable growth due to the fact that this will promise the reward settlement is kept, and it might also increase as the years pass. This is not a warranty. Something that investors need to understand is that a company that is known for being able to provide credible rewards to its investors and these returns expand with time, will certainly work really tough to stay clear of pulling down its investors. This is the type of firm to watch out for.
A financier needs to take a look at the previous efficiency of a firm they want so as to identify if its annual returns are what they truly want or otherwise before they can choose. This is because any type of firm which consistently pays returns that climb time after time remains in good monetary standing and these are the sort of services that generate a consistent flow of cash. You therefore need to detect a steady business; one whose supply prices seems to be much less unstable like the stock market. This suggests that you will investing your cash in a much less risky scenario, which is far better than in a company that does not ensure returns repayment.

The Compounding Benefit

Numerous financiers opt for dividend supplies since they always intend to experience the advantage of intensifying. This essentially means the capability to create some earnings, and after that reinvesting that earnings so regarding have more incomes from those incomes in the future. Returns intensifying entails reinvesting your returns in order to buy even more supply so regarding take pleasure in even more dividends in the long term.

Financiers do this due to the belief that when given time, cash can grow so much and also this a lot more so when you are reinvesting the little profits you obtain every quarter. It indicates that you have an excellent rate of return to take pleasure in if you reinvest them back to the stock if you are able to receive your dividends every 3 months.

For example: An investor acquires 100 shares in a firm at $50 each. This indicates that his overall financial investment will certainly deserve $5,000. The capitalist will be making $125 that year if the firm is to pay a returns to its financiers at a 2.5% price. If the business increases its returns every year by 5%, you will have a more valuable financial investment by the time you get to 10 years of spending particularly if the share price did not transform, or it rose and you reinvested your rewards back into the supplies.

To be able to take advantage of compounding, a financier requires a main investment, time and obtained incomes which are then reinvested.

The Dividend Reinvestment Plan (DRIP).

The DRIP normally a plan that a business offers in order to allow those that have shares to reinvest instantly when they receive their dividends so as to obtain more shares on the date that returns are to be paid. If you want to fully experience the compounding benefit, this will certainly be your possibility. You will certainly not get an income from the firm on the day its returns will certainly be paid yet rather, the board that is handling the strategy will certainly place the cash into the firm for you to straight acquire additional shares for you.

The majority of these DRIPs will permit capitalists to reinvest their dividend back into the business free of charge and in some cases at a price that is lower than the existing cost of shares. They are normally managed directly by the company. Some of the plans will even enable investors to purchase more shares right from the business to make sure that they can delight in excellent discount. This is what makes this kind of investing a great one to go with because at the end of everything, you will incur much less expense than you would if you were to get more shares outside the plan.

Chapter 3: Buying Dividend Paying Stocks

You have to take the step of obtaining them if you are interested in spending in returns paying stocks. Individual stocks can be acquired all the same manner in which other supplies are gotten, that is via a broker and also perhaps directly from the business itself. Investors using brokers need to companion with the most effective brokers that can recommend the very best stocks in the marketplace, and this, together with your own study searchings for can aid you make the very best selection of supplies to purchase.

Capitalists require to understand that private stock is not the only option available nor is it the very best one to consider those that wish to buy returns paying stocks. Some financiers spend through a mutual fund and this helps them in a lot of methods, amongst them being able to diversify their portfolio by allowing them to spread their financial investment across a variety of different possible stocks. The other advantage you obtain from this is that you have the ability to keep the broker charge to a minimal level.

Purchasing and also Managing Your Dividend Portfolio.

Buying simply one kind of supply is not a great idea. Financiers are motivated to spread the risk in other stocks and also this is where building as well as managing your profile will certainly begin. There are many approaches one can take in order to have their own personal stock portfolio working and also running. Many individuals will ask why this is important. A profile of returns supplies is more than the variety of supplies you have in overall; it does a great deal much more. Every financier has a preference of how their profile must look depending on the type of diversity one intends to opt for. What you need to recognize is that at the end of all of it, your portfolio must aid you construct riches in the long run. This means that your selection of supplies ought to always be the very best.

Particular variables will certainly be considered when one is developing his supply dividend profile and also these are:.

1. Your goals: The most important point you require to think about when you are investing in returns supplies is exactly what you want to accomplish. Do not think that all profiles use the exact same thing. Yes, they offer an easy revenue and also they can develop you wide range.

for many years yet you require ahead up with your special portfolio that is different from what other people are developing, based on your objectives in life. Below are points that will help you determine your option:.

The sort of return you are searching for Your level of threat resistance.
Your experience in investing.
The length of time you want to invest in dividend stocks The amount of time you have to learn more regarding supplies.

2. The return target: An ordinary portfolio split return will certainly be the next significant consideration after your objectives. The ordinary yield that you will go with ought to suffice to make sure that you will certainly obtain an excellent return of your investment every single time returns are being paid. You will most definitely consider greater yields if you are intending to use the returns pay as your revenue for your individual needs. If on the various other hand you wish to appreciate a good return after many years of investing, you will fret much more regarding returns growth as well as probably a high amount of returns.

3. Stick to your core proficiencies: Investors are expected to have a sensibly varied profile yet it is popular that you can not be an expert in every little thing. There is that location that you recognize a lot about and this is the location a lot of financiers fit purchasing. The problem is that if your stocks remain in just one or at the very least two industries, one unforeseen kip down the market can influence your profile at the same time and also you will certainly shed so much. That is why you require to diversify a little more. Develop a few more markets that you have a concept of what they have to do with. You can find out a thing or more regarding a few other industries also, to make sure that you are at least investing in sectors that you are familiar with. If you have the ability to expand in different markets, you might never ever be highly impacted even when there is a recession, given that it can not affect all sectors at the same time.

4. Invest with social obligation in mind: Investors have the choice to identify the kinds of firms they will have in theory profiles and also those that are not admitted there. Do not be the kind of investor that enables anything in their profile as long as there is wish for some dividend by the

end of the year. This is what investing with social duty in mind is all about. When you are investing, every person has their very own concepts in life as well as these should be the assisting aspects. You require to set standards that business need to come on order to match your profile. This will certainly provide you assurance given that you will certainly know that the companies that you have actually purchased are truly deserving.

5. Conduct extensive research: Now that you have a concept of what you wish to have in your portfolio, you can begin creating it. Nowadays, financiers have the advantage of the web, therefore you can utilize it to obtain all the information you might need in order to determine the best stocks that will be included in your profile. Try Yahoo Finance as an example and you will certainly locate a few of the most important firms that you can purchase. Some sites will even enable you to screen via the very best supplies in the market in order to create a much less complex checklist to select from. Keep an eye out for sites that will assist you to make stock choices with much simplicity. Benefit from what the internet is using ahead up with a great portfolio that you will certainly more than happy with for a long period of time.

6. Beginning tiny and develop your profile with time: When it concerns investing, you ought to not invest all your money at the same time. Since you already recognize what business to invest in, you need to do it wisely. Investors generally purchase two primary ways; the clumsy method as well as the elegant method. To be a clever financier, I make certain you will certainly opt for the elegant method of investing. This entails starting with a little amount of money, after that developing your setting slowly with time. Make the most of balancing out your acquiring price over a given time period as it includes some benefits to the financier.

7. Increase the huge capacity: After beginning little, you should have the ability to identify fantastic potential after some time. As soon as you have realized that a particular investment is a good one, commit and broaden to it.

What you require in your profile are core financial investments which you can count on at whatever state of the market, intermittent financial investments as well as also the little investments. All terrific standing business that have been in the market for a long period of time, those that pay their dividends well as well as promptly whatsoever times as well as have the ability to stay strong also throughout recession must be your core financial investments. Intermittent firms are much more like the core firms yet these ones are a little unstable. The tiny business are those that will need your full-time attention. You require to have just a couple of to ensure that you will certainly be able to closely check them.

Chapter 4: The Benefits of Investing in Dividend Stocks

Investors always have a difficult time deciding on the kind of financial investment to choose. Info that is around the net nowadays, in economic journals and financial investment magazines is not aiding a lot, simply due to the fact that there is too much of it and there are some inconsistencies. Whereas the majority of the investment alternatives guarantee some type of go back to investors, reward stock financiers are always trying to find their very own sort of benefits. You need to recognize that the cash is your own, as a result you need to not allow anyone make a decision for you what you ought to do with it.

To make a well educated decision of whether this is the ideal path you intend to take or not, you ought to go through the advantages in detail as well as the negative aspects as well. Examine in detail to make sure that what the financial investment is using is just what you are trying to find. You must have the ability to determine if the advantages surpass the disadvantages as this is what will assist you make the decision.

Here are the benefits you obtain from investing in dividend paying supplies.

1. There are 2 ways to win.

When it comes to returns supplies, capitalists win in two primary methods; when the share rate increases and also when you get a returns payment, which is a portion of the revenues of the business. This implies that the chances of appreciating high yearly returns are high when it concerns returns supplies. Given that there are two ways to win, chances of losing are usually on the minimum. If for instance the share price decreases by 2% and also the returns is paid at a 5% rate, you do not shed in any way. You will just shed if the reward payment supply decreases to below 2%. Dividend stock capitalists are as a result always safer that other financiers, as an example those who just depend on the changes in share cost to obtain something.

2. A constant income guarantee.

Several financial investments in the world today do not give you a revenue until you market..

This usually takes a long time considering that your broker has to search for a customer and wait to obtain a great price in order to understand an earnings for you. This is not the same with returns stocks. The dividends are paid in money by the end of the financial year. They are not paper revenues as well, which could go away right into the bearish market any type of min. This is money that you reach pocket and usage as you please. This is also cash that no person can remove from you once it has been paid out. There are business that pay their rewards quarterly as well as this suggests that you will certainly be ensured of some cash after every 3 months.

3. An opportunity to accomplish earnings plus possession
Not many investments will certainly provide you the benefits of appreciating profits as well as at the same time an opportunity to own part of business. The only option you have if you are in demand of some revenues is to offer your shares if you have invested in stocks that do not pay dividends. This will be a bad suggestion if the business has wonderful possible for growth and you may be losing your opportunity to appreciate wonderful benefits in the future. As soon as you spend in a reward paying stock, this worry will certainly not be with you. You get to settle for the profits while still your ownership continues to be undamaged. Once the company begin expanding, you are assured of even more earnings and a greater funding gratitude for you by the end of a certain amount of time. This is something to actually choose.

4. Funding gains
Returns supplies are the sort of stocks that provide the most effective capital gains in the stock market. Lots of people have a tendency to believe that all reward stocks expand slowly and consequently, they produce really little funding gains for their financiers. This may be true to some level but it is additionally real that a lot of the stocks that have signed up high funding gains in the recent past are reward supplies. This constantly depends upon the kinds of stocks that you will purchase. It is excellent to recognize exactly how the share price of a particular company is performing and exactly how it has been carrying out in the past in order to make an excellent decision of whether to invest in that company or not to ensure that you will certainly get to appreciate this and also much more advantages.

5. Delight in the benefits of intensifying
Compounding is perhaps one of the most important term worldwide of investing.

It makes certain that your investment doubles up prior to your very own eyes, without the firm needing you to put more cash into your investment. This overcomes reinvesting back your reward. You do not have to pocket your returns examine every 3 months; let the company repossess the cash and reinvest it back right into business. Ultimately, you get extra shares of that same amount. The returns quantity is not generally a lot cash, but by the end of a few years, you can picture just how much money you will have reinvested back right into the business to get more profits. This is one possibility that just returns supply financiers reach take pleasure in.

6. Dividend stock financiers are generally secure from inflation
There is absolutely nothing that terrifies capitalists greater than inflation. Many people lose a lot money to rising cost of living. Financial investment consultants will certainly always inform you that a person means through which you can maintain inflation from impacting your financial investment profits is with buying returns supplies. This is due to the fact that returns have the ability to keep pace with rising cost of living. When the share rates increase for instance, revenues that firms make tend to climb also and this indicates that you will get a higher dividend payment by the end of the arranged period. If the costs fall on the other hand, you still get some reward just that the share cost could influence your overall yearly earning if the share cost goes listed below the buying rate. The bottom-line is, you do not shed completely.

7. The buying as well as holding benefit
One thing that can be stated regarding dividend stock financiers is that they are more committed than most financiers. They usually invest for long term benefits as well as except a quick possibility to pocket some profits. They are the kind of investors that will adhere to a firm for a long period of time, in order to enjoy the profit paid both in great times and also in negative times. That is why they are seldom affected by adjustment on the market like rising cost of living.
There are supplies that just offer funding appreciation when the rates of the share rise. When the costs begin to fall, these do not ensure a financier a favorable return especially. That is why numerous investors do not hold onto such stocks for a very long time. This is the reason numerous financiers these days are selecting these sort of stocks. When you purchase as well as hold, you may take pleasure in many benefits in the future, which is something terrific to hold onto.

Chapter 5: The High-Yielding Dividend Stocks

One of the things that you require to referred to as a returns supply investor is what a reward return is. Essentially talking, dividend return is a proportion which indicates the amount of money a company pays out in returns yearly relative to its share rate. This is generally in portion form. The formula organization individuals utilize to compute the reward yield is as shown:

Dividend return= annual rewards per share/price per share

The yields for an existing year can be estimated create the previous year's returns or by utilizing the quarterly yield, then multiplying it by 4. The end result is after that divided by the existing share rate.
The dividend yield is essentially utilized to determine the capital that you will be getting for the money that you have bought the firm. Without considering the capital gains, the returns return will certainly give you the real return on your investment. This is the percent of your investment that you should be anticipating to get at the end of every year.

The High-Yielding Dividend Stocks
If the stocks of a particular company are truly the appropriate ones to invest in or not, financiers make use of the returns yield in order to identify. An investor that calls for a minimal stream of capital from his financial investment portfolio can obtain this sort of cash flow by targeting supplies that pay greater and much more steady dividend returns. These high dividend returns in some cases comes at a price of the supplies development capacity.
This is the reason all money the business is paying as dividend is money that it is not spending back right into the firm. Those companies that pay a lower returns return reinvest part of theory returns back into the business and this is what comes with fantastic capital gains for the financiers. This indicates that the firm is not making sufficient funding gains in the end. The only possibility you need to get much more from the business is the gain for holding a supply. As soon as the value of your supplies go up, you can be certain that you will certainly gain so much in returns but as long as you are obtaining a high returns yield, you can be certain that the various other benefits drop.

Numerous points must pertain to your mind when you come across a company that is paying high rewards to its investors. The firm could be underestimated then and this is something to think about prior to you choose to spend into it. This can also be a plan for the firm to attract financiers. Business that pay little dividends or no returns at all are those that are miscalculated or those that wishes to grow their capital. There are firms though, which will pay a high returns to investors, yet they are not underestimated. These are well established business, and also they are constantly the ideal options when you are searching for somewhere to spend your cash.

It is very important for an investor to consider reward returns of business that they are purchasing ahead of time in order to determine the future returns of those companies. You can use the current yearly reward repayment to establish this, or you can take the most recent quarterly repayment, then you multiply it by 4 in order to approximate the existing returns yield of that firm. Always know that the future reward repayments of companies are always unclear, consequently you will certainly never get an appropriate price quote. That is why supply investing is an extremely dangerous event that should be finished with a lot of care.

Safest means to invest in high-yielding dividend stocks
The investment globe is rather difficult. The fundamental rate of interests of financiers are returns and also safety and security as well as these passions are constantly in an inverted connection. This suggests that you either go with returns as well as risk your security or you go with the safety and ignore the returns. The trouble is that capitalists are constantly aiming to attain both, which is feasible yet not really simple. Everybody is seeking a high-yielding as well as low-risk investment, which will certainly give them advantages on both sides. Financial professionals would certainly love to offer capitalists just what they want, and they are attempting very hard to package investment items that will certainly provide both security as well as excellent returns. If therefore you are searching for high-yielding dividend supplies that are risk-free, you might be fortunate. You however need to define and be clear concerning what you mean by high and also risk-free yielding.

Safe is quite family member. Safe could indicate a financial investment that will certainly have absolutely no descending threat, and you might not find anything to invest in when it comes to reward supplies. In as much as there are great advantages in purchasing returns supplies, the danger is inescapable. You can minimize the threat if you do not place all your cash in just one company. Make the most of common funds as an example particularly those that are fixated companies with high-dividend returns. With these, you never shed completely when the firm is influenced by market problems.

Chapter 6: Avoidable Mistakes Dividend Stock Investors Make

Capitalists make mistakes regularly. Even the most knowledgeable financier, that has taken some time to study the marketplaces really well can make an awful mistake. The poor feature of investment mistakes is that they are extremely expensive. You might be sorry for ever before making them as well as this can go on for a long while. It is great to be on the lookout for several of the pricey and also usual mistakes that you might make like any kind of other capitalist to ensure that you will certainly take care regarding them. In this manner, you could spend and also enjoy your decisions after that. A few of these errors are explained right here:

1. Going with high yields: This is an extremely typical mistake in financial investment and also it is a trap that almost all investors opt for. The returns of a company can be truly attractive as well as a financier might forget all other crucial factors just because a company registered good returns. Due to the fact that you are not spending in the business for brief term benefits, the monetary health of a business should matter much more. Consider the sustainability of the dividend also to ensure that you will be getting something for the years that you will certainly buy that company.

2. Disregarding feasible future dividend development: The importance of research prior to spending helps you to identify the pattern at which the business is going so that you will certainly recognize its possible efficiency years ahead. This is very essential. You do not intend to get the exact same reward settlement you got this year twenty years to come. You require to buy a business that has a likelihood of boosting its dividends payout over the years. Invest in the best firm. Possibilities that its share rate will at some point increase along with its rewards are high.

3. Falling short to diversify: This has actually been talked about previously in this book. Diversity aids a capitalist to spread the risk to make sure that you will certainly not lose every little thing in case of a trouble. Market conditions change and they may influence your investment. Chances of

shedding your investments will be high if the 2 markets are impacted by the market problems if you have spent in just one or two industries. Besides, you want to appreciate what various other sectors are using, for that reason purchase more fields.

4. Disregarding the results: After spending, lots of financiers do not focus on what will take place thereafter. Their primary issues comes to be the returns they are expecting at the end of a particular amount of time. If you are not mindful, this can lead to your failure. You need to classify your supplies so regarding know which ones call for even more interest than the others. If you have actually made the ideal choice, you require to keep examining what is happening in the market to determine. If there are stocks that will start to do far better, you devote to them and if there are those that are not doing so well, you give them your total interest to be able to make the right decisions when the time will come.

Conclusion

Returns stocks are absolutely a good concept for many capitalists that are figured out to experience the benefits of passive earnings. If you are a novice in reward stocks as well as you would intend to make an excellent financial investment to appreciate great returns of your cash, you have to find an excellent stock to buy. You need to learn points by yourself also, for example exactly how returns are shared out and exactly how supplies make dividends. You ought to seek information regarding the fees connected with trading on returns supplies. This essentially indicates that you need to get directly entailed with everything in order not to be sorry for the decisions that you will make.

Be prepared for what you find out as well and also attempt to think of the benefits that you get versus the dangers entailed. You need to go for it if the benefits are more than the risk. Several financiers will certainly pick to pursue fully grown companies, whose share cost is sluggish climbing, understanding far too well that they will certainly take pleasure in a consistent revenue in terms of reward from the business. Whatever the selection you will make, you need to get the real photo, thinking of feasible adjustments that can take place in future.

The benefit investors have today is that there are numerous devices that can assist you iron out healthy and balanced as well as unhealthy companies. This is just what you require in order to place your money in a financial investment that you will certainly boast of.

Introduction

For any organization or endeavor to be successful, it needs to have a great leader at the helm. The leader is the individual that establishes the standards that are to be followed, so that all individuals functioning within the organization have someplace they can draw information from, along with advice and also inspiration to help them attain their objectives.

An exceptional leader is able to drive the team ahead, so that business can grow from the within out. In the past, it was thought that the best leaders had specific characteristic, and that without those traits, leaders would certainly not succeed. This idea has been eliminated in modern as it is thought that any character type can be a leader. Leaders are developed with their qualities, which are often geared towards being charismatic as well as objective oriented. Leaders need to have expertise as well as knowledge to ensure that they can be appreciated by their followers. They likewise need to be welcoming and friendly, to make sure that the people they work with can talk to them about any kind of concerns or challenges they are encountering in the work environment. They will certainly have the ability to influence a group to attain a vision for the company, which is what will aid with its growth.

This publication is what you require as a leader, whether you are upcoming or experienced. By the time you finish it as well as use its sound guidance, you will find that leading your group to success is seamless, and you accomplish the results that you desire.

Chapter 1: The History of Motivation

Long time back, when people discussed inspiration it generally boiled down to just how much money a person was earning for the work that they do. Due to the fact that there is a benefit that they would receive for their payment, the idea was that the single reason people go to function or join a team is. Theoretically, this makes ideal sense, though it begins to handle a various note when one is dealing with the real circumstance on the ground.

It ended up that somebody can gain an amazing pay, and also yet, they are not motivated to do their jobs. If reimbursement was not the concern, then what could be the problem? It all boiled down to management, and how a leader might influence the workplace.

Leaders after that took some steps to much better recognize the people that they were leading, so that they would certainly understand what was to be done to motivate them. There were two types of motivation that were uncovered. The very first is known as inherent motivation, and also the other is extrinsic inspiration. Inherent motivation is all about what motivates an individual from the inside, which is the motivation that seems to be essential to an individual. It takes a look at the way a person approaches their own desires, and describes what they agree to do to fulfill those wishes. It is this inspiration that has the largest effect on the high quality of work that an individual creates, and also the manner in which they have the ability to engage with individuals that they are collaborating with. Individuals who are motivated inherently have the ability to appreciate their work more, as well as will certainly be pleased with their efficiency.

With external motivation, a leader will certainly need to be knowledgeable about any external factors that might inspire a team as well as encourage them to satisfy their defined objectives. These can consist of guaranteeing that they obtain a great pay packet, as well as potentially rewards when they meet the objectives that have actually been defined for them. Another kind of external motivation is based upon the worry of what would take place if the individual shed their work. This shows that this sort of inspiration may be positive in addition to negative.

When dealing with a group, a leader requires to establish what inspires each member of the group from a external and also intrinsic viewpoint, and after that, it will certainly be easier to assemble a prepare for total inspiration. This publication looks at motivation from the inherent viewpoint, relocating far from the presumption that the very best method to encourage individuals is to merely provide even more money. By creating much deeper connections with motivation, and making certain that all the participants of the team have their inherent needs satisfied to their contentment, it is thought that the only point the team can accomplish is success, which is as a result of the management they receive.

Chapter 2: Listen, Communicate and Take Action

Why would you need a leader? Well, it is because mostly all job is completed with the assistance of a group. Groups unite a series of skills and also expertise, as well as when this is integrated with energy, it is possible for a group to realize whatever they are implied to. For the best outcomes, the group needs to have guidance and direction of an effective leader, and also this leader will motivate the group to aid them reach greatness.

You need to begin by guaranteeing you recognize specifically what they require in order to get the task done when you start working towards inspiring your team. As a leader, you will certainly have a suggestion of things from a logistical angle, nevertheless, there is much more that enters into comprehending your group. So, what is it that you require to do? Here are some key points which you need to consider: -

Listen

Discover to listen to what your team is telling you. Lots of people within a company whine that they are not listened to. This does not imply that the leader is not listening to what they state, it might be that the listening is passive as well as there is no phone call to action that comes from it. There are lots of ways that your group can interact to allow you understand what they require. The first is straight ahead, where they come to you as well as straight allow you recognize what they actually need. Then, you can hang out listening to the way that they speak and also the words that they are claiming. From tone and also web content, you can recognize various requirements, especially if you find that they are not able to ask you directly. Furthermore, you must 'listen' or observe their non-verbal cues when connecting. This will help you differentiate in between dissatisfaction, unhappiness, happiness or perhaps temper when interacting with those that are under you at the job place.

Listening makes it possible for a leader to establish connections that are based upon loyalty, count on and openness. It is an indicator that you as a leader have rate of interest in what is occurring with your employees as well as you wish to aid ease their problems.

Ask for Input

After you have actually listened to your employees, you need to request their input to ensure that you can consider their ideas for the improvement of the job area. This is a manner in which you can inspire through partnership by making certain that the followers within a company believe that any kind of details that they share is appreciated. This will certainly encourage them to take part fully in what is taking place in the company, as well as also urge them to continually provide their input and also recommendations for continued renovation. When requesting for input, ask penetrating inquiries as well as consider exactly how you can best apply workable services.

Act

Once you have listened and also comprehended what the group needs from you, you will be entrusted to act on these requirements. People within a team are motivated when they really feel that they have actually been heard, and also what they have to state comes up with a call to activity. This implies that as a leader you should become engaged with your employees. After you have obtained their input, provide extra motivation by helping them expand their perspective as well as find a remedy. When they have made an effort to do so, adhere to up with them to see exactly how they are doing, as well as to show that you have an interest in their result. This reveals that you are eager and alert to recognize your workers.

Program Concern

A leader who appreciates what is occurring with their followers will certainly reveal worry. This does not imply that there ought to be constant heart to heart conversations or that the leader probes endlessly into the specialist and individual life of a fan. What it does mean is that the leader will certainly prolong some common courtesy to the fans, such as welcoming them in the early morning when getting here to function, asking inquiries regarding just how they are coping or doing with their workload, and also providing encouragement when they are facing difficulties. This type of initiative from a leader shows that the leader cares about the follower, which will encourage the employer to continue working as well as grow the link. In addition, offering appreciation to a worker makes them feel as though they count and also their payment is important for the organization.

Express Yourself Properly

Part of communication for a leader lies in the way that they are able to share themselves when confronted with hard scenarios. When dealing with annoyed workers who may place stress on the leader as well as make them really feel as though they are on the edge, this is specifically important. If they reveal that they are worried regarding the irritations of the workers by sharing their very own beliefs about a certain situation, a leader will certainly motivate their workers to interact extra successfully. While some people might believe that this shows an indication of weakness, in actual reality, it reveals that the leader can be human and at risk, qualities that fans can connect to.

Approve Others

Component of doing something about it is approving that the members of your group might intend to do points in such a way that is various from you. Everyone has an unique way that they do points, as well as a blunder that some leaders make is neglect other individuals's distinctions and try to mold and mildew them right into someone that is much like them. To encourage your team, listen to what they state and after that allow them to reveal themselves in the best way that they know exactly how. Welcome the various styles and also methods made use of to obtain job done, and as a leader you will certainly come off as compassionate and also compassionate. This will inspire your people to reveal themselves freely and also to be genuine in what they are doing.

In approval of others, there is additionally judgement, something that leaders need to prevent. A leader that is judging an individual's words or actions is one who has quit paying attention properly. When a leader is being judgmental, they will certainly commonly slam their team in an extreme manner which creates atmospheres of bitterness in the company. This also implies that people are less going to offer their all to their work. Leaders who judge others disclose themselves to be premature, as well as incapable to embrace the differences of individuals who compose their team. Rather than judge a staff member, a leader can make the effort to recognize their activity, as well as where possible, find out something from the employee.

By taking time to listen and take action based on what you have listen to with your team, you inspire them as they will feel like they are valued. This is likewise a way that you can highlight their finest strengths.

Chapter 3: Provide Controlled Freedom and Respect

Good leaders empower the people that work for them by allowing them to explore their talents and expand their potential. To motivate followers effectively, a leader needs to have some key personality traits. These are explained in this section.

People First

There would be no team or organization without the people who are working or participating to run these entities. Therefore, when looking at controlled freedom and respect, you need to begin by respecting the people within your team enough to put them first. When working in a customer oriented environment, a common mantra that is heard is that the customer should always come first. However, the customer cannot receive any service unless the employees are there to give it.

Putting your people first should be done by ensuring that they are well trained and fully equipped with what they need to get the job done. It also requires you to have a sharp focus on everything that is happening with members of the team, so that as a leader, you can identify any challenges that arise and deal with them in record time. Being attentive in this way will help you gain the respect of the people that you must work with.

Be a Visionary

There needs to be some direction within the organization so that staff know what they are working towards. This is what being a visionary entails. The leader has to have the ability to clearly communicate what is meant to happen to the organization, and to translate that vision through clear communication to every member of the team. This will help team members define for themselves how they want to grow within the organization, and also to identify where they are able to make the most useful contribution.

Create a Conducive Workplace

The layout of the workplace can have a huge effect on the motivation and cohesion of a team. If you want to motivate your teal to work together, you need to have a space that encourages unity. Modern leaders are choosing to get closer to their followers by embracing open plan offices where they are not separated from the rest of their staff by walls and doors.

In addition to being accessible, a good leader will ensure that the workplace is clear and that it has information that stimulates the people who are working. This will ensure that people are in the right mood due to their environment, which will motivate them to work towards meeting their goals, and reduce the opportunities that they have to complain.

Avoid Micromanaging

Leaders are given hefty responsibilities and are often held accountable for the results that emerge. This causes them to want work to be done perfectly, leading to a flaw in leadership that can discourage a team. That flaw is micromanaging. When a leader micromanages their team, they give the impression that they do not trust those who are working with them, and also, that this comes through as second guessing the decisions of others who are working towards the same goals. It also limits the team members from using the best of their abilities to get a job done.

To motivate people, a leader should provide information on the goals to the team members, and then give them the room to figure out how these goals should be achieved. This will have team members thinking creatively, and competing amongst each other to arrive at the best result. The quality of work that is produced when people have the freedom to work increases, and the organization is able to grow.

Set Goals which are Clear

For people to exercise the right freedom within the organization, they need to have goals which are clear. Leaders can demotivate their staff by wasting their time, especially when it is becomes challenging to discern which work is a priority and what can be done at a later date. Lack of clarity means that methodologies can get mixed up and this can result in those who are carrying out tasks making costly mistakes which are not entirely their fault. A   leader who chooses to motivate the team will make sure that everyone is clear about the goals that need to be accomplished, and the role that each member of the team needs to play so that the goals are met.

Allow Self Expression

When you are a leader, you should be highly knowledgeable about everything to do with the organization that you are working for or team that you are leading. This could lead to arrogance, where a leader places themselves on a pedestal above everyone else in the organization.

Allowing others to express themselves freely shall motivate them in their work. This means that when they are speaking, even if the leader believes that they know better, they should not interrupt their speech or ideas. This proves that the leader is willing and able to listen, and will help them earn respect.

Pay Attention to Company Policies

Leaders work under a set of rules, which they ensure are enforced and upheld by every member who is underneath their leadership. Rules and regulations are excellent for maintaining control, but, when they are not well thought out they can lead to dissatisfaction with employees. When employees are not satisfied, the results can be seen in their work, and as long as the rules remain the way that they are, it may become impossible to motivate a team. As a leader, you need to be in a position to make changes to the rules if you notice that they are not serving your purpose sufficiently. This is so that you can foster an environment of satisfaction, which will help those who are under your leadership identify opportunities and seek further development. This increases their overall motivation and their sense of purpose in the work they do.

Enable Problem Solving

A part of leadership involves settling disputes and solving problems. In any project or team there is always something that can go wrong, and the leader who tries to put out all the fires on their own will end up physically and emotionally spent, which could affect their performance. For the purpose   of motivation, the leader should allow the members of the team to sort out their own problems, by simple offering basic guidance and a reminder of what the ultimate goal for the tasks at hand should be. This will ensure that only the biggest problems are brought to the leader, and other people will be motivated to solve their own problems in an amicable way to ensure the continuation of the team.

Have a Little Fun

Finally, you can motivate your team to achieve their goals by having a little fun while in the workplace. A good leader will be able to find a balance between having fun, and not taking work as seriously as it should be taken. Leaders can make the decision to have one day of the week where people dress down and express their personalities, such as a casual dress Friday. Dressing up for certain holidays such as Halloween and Christmas could be allowed, so that employees benefit from the cheer and positivity that can be created within the work environment.

Chapter 4: Push Them to Achieve More

As a person becomes a part of a team or an employee in an organization, they are given a job description that tells them what it is they are supposed to do – it spells out their roles and responsibilities. Most people will do the bare minimum that is required from a day to day basis, which is fine if the intention is simply to try and meet organizational goals.

A good leader will realize that the bare minimum is not enough. Getting the staff to step up their game will drive the organization to unprecedented success, and therefore, they need to be motivated to achieve more. This will require a push, as employees are often comfortable with putting in minimum effort to accomplish their own goals. Here is what a leader can do: -

Believe in the Team

Every team has an objective that they are working towards, and goals which are set to help guide them. Those who are in leadership need to be in agreement with these goals if they hope to motivate the team and push people to action. This is because a leader communicates with more than just their words, as body language has much to say as well. Therefore, if you are nodding yes, but your face and demeanor are saying no, then your team will pick up that you do not trust what is happening and you will find it difficult to get them to follow through on what is expected. Leadership can only push others further if they are truly dedicated to what is happening for the team, and they believe in the goals that have been set out for accomplishment. Their peaceful and determined state of mind will be easily picked up and everyone else in the team will react to that.

Make them Happy

How do people behave when they are happy? They do more, the surpass expectations and they elevate an organization. To motivate a team so that they can be happy, positive and enthusiastic requires an astute and observant leader. Ensure that the work environment has all the tools that they employees need, and that they are encouraged towards working and meeting their goals. It is also key to pay attention to an employee who upset the balance that you are working to create. When someone is not happy, they can quickly spread their negative mood, so a good leader should find a way to restore them to happiness. This shows the other employees that you care about the team, which will motivate them to work freely, knowing that they are important enough to warrant concern and attention.

Be Careful about Punishment

Typically, when someone does something wrong, the jerk reaction of a leader would be to punish them so that they learn a lesson and never repeat the mistake. This has proven to work in many circles, though it is highly dependent on the type of punishment that is given out. When motivating a team, it is crucial to realize that people will make mistakes from time to time and these mistakes provide an excellent opportunity for learning. Rather than give out a punishment that could lead to demotivation, choose to motivate by giving some encouragement, and ensuring that the employee has a second chance to work towards making things right.

Spend Time Wisely

Many leaders believe that they have to check in with the members of their team to ensure that the work is getting done as expected. This often results in creation of meetings, which take up a considerable amount of time and do not always have excellent results. Motivation occurs when people are actually doing their jobs rather than talking about what they should be doing. Planning is necessary, but the way it is done can help with ensuring that there are positive results. Therefore, as a leader, when you want to have a meeting, ensure that all those who are attending actually need to be there, rather than inviting every single person in a department. The agenda of the meeting should be sent to everyone before the meeting takes place, and time management should be adhered to. By the time the meeting has been concluded, all those who were in attendance should be clear about what is expected of them and the actions that they need to take.

In the process of pushing the people in your team to achieve more, there is something that you need to recognize as a leader. You can motivate a member of your team by taking all the right actions as have been mentioned so far, but, for there to be success, that member of the team also needs to shoulder part of the responsibility for self-motivation. What you need to do as a leader to help a person achieve more is ensure that they are in an environment that is supporting, and speaks to what intrinsically motivates them. This will ensure that the individual is motivated and has a positive attitude, seeing as they are better able to meet their goals.

Chapter 5: Develop Future Leaders

This all begins when the leader is working towards creating a cohesive team, and takes the time to identify with every person that he has to work with. In order to develop future leaders, special attention must be paid to the relationship between the leader and the follower.

Every follower will require some positive one-to-one interaction to bring out their best qualities. This means that the leader must humble themselves so that they can communicate with the follower and create an emotional connection. Once a follower understands that they can relate with their leader, then they are more motivated to work at their best. This is because they know that any hurdles they face can easily be addressed, and also believe that having a personal connection means that they can count on the leader for the required support.

Encourage Self-Development

People within an organization can become motivated if they know that the hard work they put in will pay off. There are members within a team who are always looking towards the future, planning their career progression over the next three or more years. A good leader will nurture and encourage them, understanding the value that they are able to add to the organization. To further motivate them, they should be given opportunities to train and learn so that they are able to develop new skills which are beneficial to the organization. It is also important that a leader follows through in rewarding people who have earned the right to advance within the organization. When others realize that advancement is a real possibility, they will become more motivated to grow as well.

Examine the Individual

The process of developing a leader depends highly on the type of person that you are grooming for the future. You need to take into account their personality traits, strengths and weaknesses, and also determine how they could provide a worthy contribution with their skills. This means that you cannot use a one size fits all approach to future leadership – you need to examine each person as an individual. How this motivates people is that it shows them the leader actually sees who they really are, is able to observe them and appreciate what it is that they have to offer. It also acknowledges the differences that people have, and shows that the leader is willing to think through decisions so that everyone is placed in teams or leadership positions that are best suited to their unique circumstance.

Try Transformational Leadership

There are many different types of leadership styles, but one that has proven to be highly motivational is transformational leadership. This is the type of leadership that looks to the future, and gets people to work towards creating a future that is meaningful for them and for the organization or team. It motivates people as it opens up the doors for them to start working towards the extraordinary, and this drive helps followers trust their leaders, and show their motivation as an expression of their loyalty. A transformational leader will get those who are within the team to work towards meeting their future goals by providing guidance over tasks and ensuring that the relationships that are created within the team are strong and can be sustained for the long run. The transformational leader motivates by being a role model, sparking enthusiasm and helping a team find balance.

Recognize Achievement

By the time you are working towards preparing a member of your team as a future leader, they should have proven that they can handle the responsibility, or have traits that make them stand out from everyone else as a potential leader. To further motivate them, you should recognize their achievements, especially when they have proven that they are able to meet their stipulated goals. This can be done by acknowledging a job well done in writing, or where possible and ethical, giving them a reward in the form of a gift. By offering rewards, which are unexpected, you motivate the person to work harder. You also show them how they should treat the people that they lead in the future so that they can also have results that are the same or possibly better for the team as a whole.

Provide Team Members with Feedback

It is your responsibility as a leader to give the members of your team feedback about their performance so that they can be motivated to work towards their goals. This feedback should be constructive, telling them what they are doing right or wrong, and explaining how they can improve their performance. A leader that is able to have an honest and compassionate conversation about performance will motivated a member of the team to work harder and minimize their weaknesses. This approach is more caring then reprimanding, and provides the future leader the room to make corrections to their behavior and see how this will help them meet the stipulated goals.

Remember Ethics

The final lesson that must be taught is the importance of being ethical in business. In leadership, people are motivated when they know that their leaders have high levels of integrity and value their reputations. This also indicates that the leader will behave in an appropriate manner. This will help to motivate a team, as they can be proud of their leader and what the leader stands for. When developing a future leader, they will see firsthand the benefits of being a person that is ethical, and shall take advantage of the lessons learned to improve the way they will lead a team in the future.

Ensure that all the people who are working towards becoming future leaders understand the meaning of expectations, as this will have quite an effect on their development. Leadership that is effective often has people who understand what to expect from their leaders, and what their leaders expect from them. This makes it possible to avoid unwelcome surprises in the workplace, or to dash a person's hopes and leave them disappointed. Leaders should let their team know that they have the final decision, even though they may take into account any suggestions that are passed forward. This ensures that at the end of it all, a compassionate and empathetic leader is not taken for granted, and instead, everyone is clear on who is in charge and providing direction.

Chapter 6: Be the Best Example

The first person that a follower will look for to get inspiration is their leader, and therefore, the leader should carry out their tasks in the way that they want to be emulated. How can a leader do this and motivate their followers effectively? Here are some things that can be done: -

Elevated Expertise

The leader of a team or in an organization needs to have elevated levels of expertise so that the followers know that the leader is capable of getting the job done. That is why most people become leaders after they have managed to get some experience at the job, rather than just following an earned qualification such as a degree.

When you are knowledgeable, you can motivate your team by easily being able to point out the mistakes they are making, and offering solutions on how these mistakes can be corrected. Members of the team are given the opportunity to improve on their work, so that they can become better workers who are more effective. Workers who are more effective are able to carry out their tasks much more easily, therefore, an expert leader is an asset for any follower determined to do a good job.

Time Management

The easiest way to bring an organization down is to work with a team of people who are unable to manage their time effectively. This leads to delays in getting work down, customer disappointment, tension and anger within the workplace. A leader needs to be able to manage their own time effectively. This means arriving at the office on time or ten minutes earlier than the day is to start. It also means always arriving at meetings in time, and ensuring that agendas are followed. Furthermore, this requires for leaders to always meet their deadlines.

When a leader does all of this, a competitive and inspired follower will be determined to perform up to the standard of the leader or even to surpass them. Other staff will be motivated to work within the rules as they realize that it is not too challenging for the leader. This will help to keep them in line, and ensure that they work effectively and efficiently.

Be Accountable

Laying blame on others is disheartening to the team, and it can lead to resentment and anger when a leader fails to take responsibility when things go wrong. Many leaders are quick to allow their followers to take the fall for their own mistakes. A leader who wants to motivate a team will always be accountable for the way that the team performed, and will also be accountable for their own work.

If people within the team are not afraid of being "thrown under the bus" when there are things going wrong, they will be more likely to take responsibility for their own mistakes. Accountability ensures that the organization can move in the right direction, and encourages an honest work force.

Do Things Right the First Time

As a leader and in a position of power, you may be tempted to cut corners in order to get things done. When your followers see this, many will lose respect for you and others may even begin to emulate what you are doing, believing that they can get away with it. Leaders need to be role models, and should work in the most ethical way possible. This reveals that they have principles, and helps followers trust in them.

Develop Intense Passion

Should you want to motivate people as a leader, you must prove to them that you are passionate about what you are doing within the organization. That passionate should come from deep within you, so that you are able to exude it in the most authentic way. Your passion as a leader is the energy and force behind a successful organization, and will propel the team towards working to meet organizational goals.

Practice Mindfulness

Excellent leaders are mindful, meaning that they have learned how they should be present to everything that is happening in their surroundings. This requires a leader to be attentive to both non-verbal and verbal communication. A leader who is able to show that they are present will motivate their employees as they will be able to participate in conversations, engage in interesting dialogue and have proper comprehension of what others are saying. In addition, it communicates that the leader is authentic and aware of all that is happening in the organization. People are motivated by leaders who reveal that they are not disconnected, and being mindful is evidence that the leader is interested and ever listening to what is happening within the organization.

Leaders are the source of energy for their teams or organizations, and therefore, they bear the responsibility of maintaining positive energy. Leadership requires a person to motivate through their own passion, and to ensure that no matter what is happening within the external or internal environment in the company, they remain a beacon that others are able to depend on.

Leadership also requires a sense of balance when it comes to work and to life. Balance is in the form of taking care of oneself physically, by keeping fit and watching their health. There is also spiritual care that helps one connect with themselves deeply, which makes it easier to offer advice when necessary to the rest of the team. Finally, a leader needs to be careful with their emotions, keeping them under control when provoked or going through challenging situations in life. People who see that their leaders have established a great balance between the work place and how they manage the rest of their lives, will be motivated to do what is necessary as they trust in the stability of the leadership.

Conclusion

A quick evaluation of leadership today will bring something important to light, and that is, an employee will place more value on a leader who is strong and inspirational, then on how much money they are able to earn at a job.

Through this book, you have learned how you can use leadership to motivate people in the modern workplace. To begin with, a leader needs to be able to listen to every member of their team, taking time to understand what is being said and control their reactions. This will help the team feel empathy and compassion from their leader, and increase the overall loyalty. They will be motivated to work hard and continuously improve their communication with the leader.

In addition, a leader should provide controlled freedom to members within a team so that they are willing to take responsibility for their work. Once they are accountable, they will be motivated to work hard and earn respect from the leader and anyone else that they are working with.

This book also explains the best ways that a leader can push others to achieve more. This is based on intrinsic motivation that comes from within, so that they are not reacting to fear. Self-motivation is sustainable and ensures that there are long term results which are beneficial.

Leadership and motivating people comes down to the way that the leader behaves themselves. The most effective thing that could be done is to take the approach that says followers should do as the leader does, meaning the leader should always set the best example.